Beauty in the Broken Places

Beauty in the Broken Places

Poems by

Cristina M. R. Norcross

© 2019 Cristina M.R. Norcross. All rights reserved. This material may not be reproduced in any form, published, reprinted, recorded, performed, broadcast, without the express written consent of Cristina M.R. Norcross. All such actions are strictly prohibited by law.

Cover design by Shay Culligan
Cover artwork by Erin Prais-Hintz. Copyright 2018

ISBN: 978-1-949229-36-3

Kelsay Books
Aldrich Press
www.kelsaybooks.com

Dedicated to the memory of Cora Jane Hassell Della Corte and her indomitable spirit of strength, determination, and faith.

Acknowledgments

I would like to extend a special thank you to the literary magazines, journals, anthologies, and other venues where some of the poems from *Beauty in the Broken Places* were first published.

Bramble: "This Passage" (2017)
The MOON Magazine: "Hold Close What Fades" (2017)
Pirene's Fountain: "Letting Go of the Shell" (2017), "You Are Limitless" (2017)
Red Cedar Magazine: "With Oval Arms" (2017)
Visual Verse: "Before We Part Ways" (2017), "We Need to Drink the Steam" (2017)
The Weekly Avocet: "To Float on Gracious Wings" (2016)
Your Daily Poem: "The Last Party" (2010)

"Breaking Bread with Chicken Booyah" first appeared in the *Bards Against Hunger Anthology: 5th Year Anniversary Edition* (Local Gems Press, 2017)

"Transcending" first appeared in *Still Life Stories* (Kelsay Books, 2016)

A small selection of poems from this collection first appeared on display in 2016, as part of a special ekphrastic art exhibit at the Q Gallery Cooperative (Stevens Point, WI). These poems were written for artist Erin Prais-Hintz's featured show called, "Beauty in the Broken Places," with visual artwork also included by other Q Gallery member artists. The journey of this book would not have been possible without the inspiration provided by the collaborative ekphasrtic art and poetry exhibit with Erin Prais-Hintz.

Contents

This Passage	11
Letting Go of the Shell	13
Mirror Dance	14
When We Twist	15
Go Find Her	17
Erasure	18
When We Meet	19
You Are Limitless	20
Transcending	21
In Search of a Good Boat	22
Your Spear of Truth	23
Before We Part Ways	24
Never Mind the Breaking	26
My Uterus Lives in Minnesota	27
Slipstream	28
A Cross Made of Scars	29
Be a Warrior of Love, Not Hate	31
The Last Party	32
Breaking Bread with Chicken Booyah	33
Holding Space	35
Hold Close What Fades	36
The Next Glimpse of Wing	37
Roadside Beauty	39
Cutting a Path	40
We Need to Drink the Steam	41
To Float on Gracious Wings	43
With Oval Arms	44
Your Sacred Candle	45

This Passage

When will you come to know
that light dances
in every strand of your luminous hair?

This passage—
this starburst pattern of lines,
casting shadows in every direction,
is not the tunnel
you think it is.

It is every alleyway,
every bike path,
every back road,
every hidden, tree castle
of wonder
you have ever wandered into.

Enchantment—
eyes blind to touch,
you dream through every
interruption,
as if this page is your slipstream—
your smooth, velvet curtain
to the other side.

This volume is slim.
There is so much more chalk dust
to powder your fingertips with.

The sky is raining words,
and you eat every last letter,
in the hopes that it leads
to your book of new names.

You put on the cape—
walk quietly into the woods—
start living
the way you long for things—
with big, greedy gulps of air.

Letting Go of the Shell

This is the story of an egg shell—
the thin sheen of white
separating the vulnerable now
from the certainty of tomorrow.

I am not this, says Perfection.
I am not enough, whispers Insecurity.

Cactus-like isolation—
the sharp paralysis of standing still—
we are unable to hear
even the closest plane flying overhead.

A milky, gauze veil falls,
when we allow light
to permeate all things.
With eagle-eyed vision,
we see the beauty of a broken branch
with the same reverence
as beach plum petals about to bloom.

So this is how we break.
So this is how we mend.

Mirror Dance

The body feels most beautiful
in its foggy-mirrored state.
Without seeing much,
I know that I am there.

Grace traces a smooth outline,
removing distinct details.
There is only movement
and shadow
in the white mist air.
Even the zippered scars
across my belly
float.
The red rubber lines become blurred—
ribbed color aspects
of a painting.

We dance together—
my nude twin and I.
Without inhibition,
I see beauty for what it truly is—
abandon
acceptance
the freedom to embrace space—
imperfectly whole.

When We Twist

Inside, my body is screaming,
but you don't want to hear
about my missing organs—
the way the skin puckers at the stitches—
the way bending or twisting
is a sword in my side.

Perhaps I should hold my words—
wrap them up in a clean, cotton cloth—
not say how it really is.
It's fine. I'm fine.
Everything is fine.

There is a potted plant
that keeps needing water.
Every time I say the word, *fine,*
the soil becomes more dry—
the leaves lose their veritas.

The heart ticks its metal gears
one spoke at a time.
It is a slow-motion exercise in movement,
like a snail oozing forward
inch by inch.

This truth you turn away from
is humanness.
It is you in 10 years.
It is your neighbor's aunt's surgery
that you didn't really want to hear about.

It is the ugly bandage
that frays and still sticks,
until ready for removal.
It is the untidiness of living
that you try so hard to forget.

Go Find Her

I'm saving a love letter for you—
for the you who only sees mirrored flaws
and faded, forgotten beauty.
I'm saving you tender words of appreciation
for the you who counts imagined mistakes
like pennies in a big glass jar—
for the you who needs to be reminded
of the sheer glory of your existence.

I'm saving a love letter for your hands—
the ones you fidget with when you worry.
Let me hold them.
Let me cover them with soft, lamb's wool gloves.

Let me celebrate what you have forgotten.
For the you who holds lack
like a beribboned brick parcel,
balanced on curved, burdened shoulders—
let me remind you that when you sing,
leaves reach in earnest, like reaching for the sun.

For the you who blooms and bends
just to provide someone the patience of
a sea of grass.
For the you who presses pause to say,
Thank you or *I see you*.
I am saving this love letter in my pocket,
in case you forget to cherish the self
who walks in Light with you—
the one who embraces the fullness of your worth.
Go find her.

Erasure

Women are disappearing.
We erase ourselves,
when we become small—
when we shed pounds,
shave off inches,
deny our Rubenesque curves.

The denial becomes the dangling carrot.
The stomach pains at night—
evidence that we are burning away
the unnecessary—
the extraneous parts of ourselves.

This melts away the you—
and the me.
This gives permission to the inner critic
to pulverize,
to damage,
to eliminate the essence.

You deserve to exist here.
You belong to the beauty of bones
and flesh—
the joy of tangling limbs—
the bounty of your body,
and all of the glorious, delicious
ways in which your belly sings—
the way your toes curl.
The way even your eyes smile,
when you know that every touch
and tumble is the sky holding a cup
of your fullness.

When We Meet

I will feed you more colorful vegetables—
more often.
(Do marinated mushrooms count?)

I will not take for granted
the house of the body—
these feet that take me places—
these eyes that see love.

I will be more gentle
with my lower back.
I will be more accepting
of changes in shape
and elasticity.

So rather than beat the 45-year-old version of me
into submission—
into some kind of cookie-cutter
magazine creation,
I am going to rejoice more.
I am going to say, *Thank you*, more.
I am going to befriend the woman
waiting to greet me at the end of the lane,
because she is offering to walk with me.
She is willing to wait for me to catch up.

You Are Limitless

There is beauty in broken places—
the parts we cling to—
the memories kept hidden
in crevices kept close.

Where Light escapes and shines,
awareness lays bare our truths.
It begins to heal
what remains hidden.

We break open.
We uncover the soft underbelly
of vulnerability—
the tender heart.

Who calls to you,
when the shadows come?
Who dwells behind the door
that is you?
The inner voice who says,
You are loved.
You are safe.
You are limitless.
This is the one, true voice.
Listen to this
above all others.

There is beauty in broken places.
There is strength in the deepest canyon.
There is beauty in every, sacred facet
that is you.

Transcending

(for Frida Kahlo)

Transcending pain—
allowing limbs to travel in another dimension,
the sweet, doleful breath of sleep.

I can only wonder
what my wellness looks like
in another world.
Moving freely,
beauty informs my every step.
My artwork sings joyfully,
instead of documenting my tired, woman's form.

I live inside the layers of color on canvas.
Trepidation only comes
when there is no easel or brush.

I live. I live. I live.

My eyes look out from orange and red campfires.
A beaded necklace frames a face of vision—
the landscape of story.
Walls covered with passion and history,
streaked with more than the heart could possibly reveal.

I share with you my secret,
like an unfurled flower in morning.
Unfold yourself.
Offer up your broken pieces
and be healed.

In Search of a Good Boat

We are all climbing rocks to the lighthouse.
The waves lap at the edges.
The clouds gather with a disapproving frown.
This is hard.
No one is helping.
Maybe we'll try another day.

I will braid you a sturdy rope with my hair,
if you could fashion some sandals from this cloth.
Could we bind our boats together?
Do you think it would work?

I see the woman with the pink hair again, today.
She is peeking at me through the subway car
with curious eyes.
She is trying to tell me about today—
about the landlord calling for the rent this morning—
about the spilled coffee,
the spilled words,
the encrusted tomato sauce on last night's plates.
Her eyes tell the tale.
I am the only one looking back.

Could we bind our boats together?
Do you think it would work?

Your Spear of Truth

You are pure air and deep water.
You are diamond shining stars.
You are dense fog and gleaming sheets of rain.
In fact, you are the whole damn sky.
You are the beauty of bare feet.
You are dry, chapped hands and a bone-tired body,
but you are more than you think you are.
You are the hot air balloon rising.
You are the first bulb pushing through the soil.
This is your strength—
your spear of truth.
Now use it.

Before We Part Ways

(inspired by the artwork of Manon Bellet)

Dear Faithful Womb,

We are saying goodbye in 2 weeks,
but I want you to know
that this letting go—
is not my giving up.
I am celebrating your half-moon shape,
your vastness,
and your delicate demeanor.
I praise your ability to expand and contract—
your blessing of two healthy sons.
Just between you and me,
you do know what a miracle you are, right?

This long road has been circuitous.
We have traveled a painful path,
and now that there is nothing left for us to weather—
nothing left to fill,
it is time to go.

I feel like I should give you a proper send off.
A proper outing?
You will be out soon enough.
Maybe we will just sit with each other
and ponder the universe within.
We have been to war with our cells,
with tissue, veins, and masses—
with cysts, fibroids, endometriosis,
IVF egg harvesting, and embryo transfers.

Just when I thought we were through
to the other side of things,
there was always something more to endure.

For that, I don't curse you—
like you might think I would.
For these miracles of pain, burden, and joy
I want to thank you for the gifts of
perseverance, patience, endurance,
quiet faith, and gentle confidence
in this wholly imperfect body—
that is also perfectly whole.

Never Mind the Breaking

Her bones turned to crystal
when the days became a lake.
Her feet found the water,
and with small steps,
she submerged all sound
and want.
She learned to communicate
with hums.
Only the deepest part of the lake
could hear her.
So, with feet planted,
she chose to soak
like a thick biscuit in milky tea.
Never mind the breaking.

My Uterus Lives in Minnesota

My uterus now lives in Minnesota,
in a research lab with my ovaries.
Or, at least, they share the same shelf space.
I expect great things from my female parts
in this afterlife.
I hope that they are embellishing things,
using colorful adjectives,
and telling the length and breadth of their stories,
with each scan and microscopic test.
I hope that they took good notes
from age 13 to 45.
Every year of treatment, hormone regimens,
and surgeries should be memorized by now.
Saying goodbye to this trio was made easier
by knowing about the curious next realm.
They are giving something back to the world
on my behalf.
They have a renewed sense of purpose.
I vaguely remember closing my eyes
and counting backwards.
Upon awakening, five sets of stitches remained.

Slipstream

I dreamt about the ocean last night—
about how it feels like
ruffled blankets—
about how it finds me
when I need to find myself.

Like an astronaut
staking his claim on discovery,
my awake brain digs the pole deep.
It allows anxiety-fueled pathways
to criss-cross
in the open night sky—
thoughts running rampant—
the spaghetti junction of every
single thing worried about today,
and every other thing I might
worry about tomorrow.

So the bubbles of prayer,
float and hover.
My starry-eyed, sleepless self
puts on a night cap
and fuzzy slippers.

Eventually, the ripples in the water
settle,
and I drift into dream—
blissful oblivion.

A Cross Made of Scars

Your scar and my scar
could form a cross—
a sculptural overlay.
The son and daughter of a priest
make a sacred sign.

I remember the day you received
your vertical marking.
One stent became a by-pass.
Then it became a double,
a triple, and finally, a quadruple by-pass.
Hours and hours passed.
I watched our father say a prayer for you
over the phone before surgery.
I made dinner for my nephew and our Dad.
We three ate meatloaf,
while we waited for you to wake up.
Dad crossed himself
after he hung up the phone.
I heard the tremble in his voice.
Grace stood beside us, stately—
quietly breathing for us,
when we could not breathe.

My marking is horizontal,
created years earlier
by the removal of internal scars—
at least the ones they could see—
tissue and zigzag lines from a life
with endometriosis.

Two babies re-opened that line.
These were joyous reasons to be opened up—
musical voices, tight hugs, spontaneous laughter.

Our scars could form a cross—
a prayer for parts lost—
a ritual for things found—
things regained.

Be a Warrior of Love, Not Hate

And by warrior, I mean—carrier.
And by carrier, I mean sacred guardian.
And by sacred guardian, I mean vessel.
And by vessel,
I mean, be an instrument of love.
And by instrument,
I mean—strum, sing, play, dance, move
to the melody of souls,
which we all know how to sing.
We just seem to have forgotten the words—
too focused on that warrior with the shield,
held up in fear of The Other.
When we take the shield away,
when we take the fear away,
when we carry within our hearts,
minds, bodies, and souls
the sacred gift that was given to us
so many moons ago,
we are left with what we came here with—
what we are all made of
in our deepest core selves—
love.

The Last Party

(for Josie)

It all begins to fade
in the land of forget-me-not years.
One moment I am dropping a slice of lemon
into my tea—
the next moment
the back of my bed raises
with the click of a magic button.

Crosswords are my saving grace.
All of the clues—
a familiar comfort.
I wonder who keeps filling them in?
She should be more considerate and use a pencil.

There is a woman who comes and points
to pictures on my dresser.
Sometimes I am good at the guessing game—
sometimes not.
She is kind though and brings me a new nightgown
with each visit.

In times of joyful suspension,
the room is filled
with people I have not seen in years.
Gertrude's fur wrap was always too showy,
but it looks good on her now.
Bill is busy serving cocktails,
while they set up another Canasta game.
It is a party of laughter and noise.
You should come—
before it all disappears.

Breaking Bread with Chicken Booyah

We sat on wooden benches
while the steam from chicken broth
left the air humid—
a rich, golden scent.
Margarine containers for bowls—
just enough to go around.

Each child's name started
with the letter J.
They had fourteen to feed,
plus our family of four.
This was generosity.

The youngest daughter
touched me on the arm,
*You wanna watch my
sister get her ears pierced
with a needle, a potato and an ice cube?*
I nervously smiled—
not knowing if this was
a serious question, but secretly thrilled
that I was invited to a sisters-only ceremony.

There was bread
and broth called, chicken booyah.
It was a true welcoming.
Soup, warmth, conversation,
and talk of sharing recipes.

This is how you greet
a neighbor—
with a chair pulled out,
napkins laid on the table,
and the knowledge
that you are home.

Holding Space

Tell me everything you know
about sorrow.
Every fragrant leaf of memory—
every fragment of absence felt—
every distant land you drift to,
when staring off into the middle distance.

I will hold space for you
between these palms—
my hands, soft parentheses.
I cannot hope to fill the gap—
the empty arms you once filled
with love.
But, I offer one thing
and will keep offering it—
empathy in the form of
my gentle punctuation marks—
to house your grief—
to give you a home,
and if nothing else,
to give you time
while holding empty space.

Hold Close What Fades

(for Ruth Ann Frauen)

Hold close what fades—
what melts in the noonday sun.
The rounded outline of love
waits for no one.
It follows the curve
of will and insistence.
It runs for the cool shadows
of early morning,
when dawn never tasted so sweet—
when new beginnings
still depend on
so much moonlight.

The Next Glimpse of Wing

It may start small,
but it doesn't end small—
this hidden ember you,
growing older, but glowing golden,
like a furnace.

The ghost outlines float.
The you from 10 years ago,
3 years ago, 2 months ago—
these are all gone.
The old you no longer breathes.
In exchange for this perpetual rebirth,
leaves drop—
enveloped by so much soil.

Falling through time,
into the cavern of memory,
the old bodies you once inhabited
disappear in layers of fog and ice.
On newly shorn wool piled high,
spirit bounces from cloud to cloud
of experience and loss.
Each landing—
a miracle of discovery.

So this is who I once was.
So this is how we say goodbye.

Candy floss and honeycomb.
Oh, to know and taste
how sweet life is.
Each connection is confection.
We lick our lips,
like contented cats,
waiting for the next glimpse of wing.

Roadside Beauty

Even roadside weeds have beauty—
the way the wind sways the taller stems
and the way color spreads like wildfire in all directions—
without pattern, structure, or guilt.

The road follows a straight line.
Lights shine in large circles,
telling us to stop, slow down, or go.
Mysterious seeds dropped by passing birds
never meant to bloom—
somehow thrive and fill the side of the road
with color.
If we stop long enough
at one of those big red circles
in the sky,
we might just notice
unexpected splashes of purple wonder.

Cutting a Path

Cutting a path through water
with your body,
you leave behind
your old skin—
the you that shivered
like a leaf,
when asked a question.

You—with the bright blue ring
and the cautious smile.
You cut through that water
with a confidence
no one knew you had,
because this swimming pool
was your Atlantis,
and you were a champion of depths.

All sounds became muffled.
Just a fraction of light
spotted the surface,
in between oak tree shadows.
You lived in that moment
before the car horn
honked your goodbyes for you,
before the lifeguard's whistle
cut through the air,
before your ears found the surface
and told you,
once again,
that you were land bound—
until next time.

We Need to Drink the Steam

(inspired by the artwork of Alejandro Alvarez)

Your throne is empty
despite a scepter made of aqua, concentric hearts.
The world spins—
it shakes its head
over the vacuum left behind,
when compassion
went packing.

We white wash the news.
We numb the senses
with liquid or pill.
But you—
you are incomparable.
Come back.
We beckon you,
in earnest,
for the chance to kneel
at your feet—
to visit the burning labradorite star
left hanging in the sky.

We retreat,
and the walls are covered in graffiti.
No full cup, spilling with blame,
can possibly cleanse this,
so we paint with our veins—
throw up our arms
and dance with eyes closed,
just to awaken the other senses.

If you listen closely,
you can hear the twelve noon bells singing.
You can smell fresh dough baking—
the white steam of it hangs in the air.
Blades of grass reach for it and drink.

To Float on Gracious Wings

We are all just burning embers
of our former years.
Our past adventures give off
smoke, like so many
tawny orange and red umber leaves,
gathered in a pile.

Long days of summer cycling,
and sand-dusted feet on linoleum floors,
give way to the swaying of trees,
from an insistent wind.
The sandhill cranes seek
distant skies of blue.

My only hope is that the cardinals
will stay a bit longer,
decorating the branches of our tall oak
with red brushstrokes.

A single dove perches
on the apex of our house—
watching and waiting.

He seems to be standing guard,
keeping the 7pm sunset at bay—
blessing our home
with a certain faithfulness
in the seasons.

We float together
on gracious wings
and watch the world
quietly walk inside.

With Oval Arms

You are the soft yawn
of a waking child.

You are the fervent rise of the orange blaze at dawn.
You are surging blood flow
and the textured pattern of strong muscles.

You are the lighthouse strobe,
when the blue-black night
blankets the sea.

You are oval arms
embracing a newborn.

You are the perpetual morning
on a night cast earth.

You are the Lightworker of today
and the energy guide of tomorrow.

You are the branch connecting
all trees, and you have love
for each and every leaf.

You come from the forest
and to the forest you will return,
when each rock is balanced,
when each cobweb connects.

Your Sacred Candle

Every life holds a singular candle.
We stand vigil for one another.
These sacred stories we share
are *our* stories—
they are *everyone's* stories.
Narratives of persistence and connection—
things broken and things shining with hope—
what we lose and what we find.

We hold close the fading Light—
knowing that the ephemeral river
will disappear and reappear.
We have faith that water will keep flowing—
that the river will never leave
the very heart of things.
It will run through our lives,
like liquid silver,
in the cracks we tend to
and mend.

About the Author

Cristina M. R. Norcross is the founding editor of the online poetry journal, *Blue Heron Review* (www.blueheronreview.com), and the author of 7 poetry collections. Her most recent books include *Amnesia and Awakenings* (Local Gems Press, 2016), and *Still Life Stories* (Kelsay Books, 2016). Her works have been published in: *The Toronto Quarterly, Red Cedar, The MOON Magazine, Your Daily Poem, Lime Hawk, Bramble, The Poetry Storehouse, Right Hand Pointing, Visual Verse,* and *Pirene's Fountain,* among others. Cristina's work also appears in numerous print anthologies. Cristina was the co-organizer of *One Vision: A Fusion of Art and Poetry* (2009-11). Cristina is currently the co-founder of Random Acts of Poetry and Art Day (Feb. 20th). Find out more about this author at: www.cristinanorcross.com

Made in the USA
Middletown, DE
20 May 2021